Analysis Trading:

All You Need to Know to Be Successful

© Copyright 2018 by All rights reserved.

The follow eBook is reproduced below with the goal of providing information that is as accurate and reliable as possible. Regardless, purchasing this eBook can be seen as consent to the fact that both the publisher and the author of this book are in no way experts on the topics discussed within and that any recommendations or suggestions that are made herein are for entertainment purposes only. Professionals should be consulted as needed prior to undertaking any of the action endorsed herein.

This declaration is deemed fair and valid by both the American Bar Association and the Committee of Publishers Association and is legally binding throughout the United States.

Furthermore, the transmission, duplication or reproduction of any of the following work including specific information will be considered an illegal act irrespective of if it is done electronically or in print. This extends to creating a secondary or tertiary copy of the work or a recorded copy and is only allowed with express written consent from the Publisher. All additional right reserved.

The information in the following pages is broadly considered to be a truthful and accurate account of facts and as such any inattention, use or misuse of the information in question by the reader will render any resulting actions solely under their purview. There are no scenarios in which the publisher or the original author of this work can be in any fashion deemed liable for any hardship or damages that may befall them after undertaking information described herein.

Additionally, the information in the following pages is intended only for informational purposes and should thus be thought of as universal. As befitting its nature, it is presented without assurance regarding its prolonged validity or interim quality. Trademarks that are mentioned are done without written consent and can in no way be considered an endorsement from the trademark holder.

Table of Contents

Introduction 1

Chapter 1: Understanding Technical Analysis 3

Chapter 2: Fundamental Analysis Primer 16

Chapter 3: Technical Indicators to Watch 26

Chapter 4: Understanding Candlestick Charts 41

Chapter 5: Consolidation Patterns to Watch..................... 49

Chapter 6: Money Management Tips 61

Conclusion 73

Introduction

Congratulations on purchasing *Analysis Trading: All You Need to Know to Be Successful* and thank you for doing so. When it comes to trading successfully, the more you know the more prepared you are for every possible outcome and the more likely you will be to turn a profit in the end. This is why analysis is so important to trading successfully, regardless of which asset you choose as without it you are doing little better than gambling.

As such, the following chapters will discuss everything you need to know in order to get started with this time-tested trading strategy, starting with an explanation of the basics of technical and fundamental analysis to ensure that you have a reliable foundation regardless of which direction you decide to go in moving forward. Next, you will learn about numerous different technical indicators to watch to ensure that no trend ever manages to take you by surprise again.

This analysis of useful indicators then continues with a discussion of how to read candlestick charts along with strategies for using them effectively. From there you will find a discussion of various consolidation patterns to be aware of and the types of signals they send as well as plenty of useful money management tips to ensure that you are able to successfully hold on to as much of your profit as possible in the long-term.

There are plenty of books on this subject on the market, thanks again for choosing this one! Every effort was made to ensure it is full of as much useful information as possible, please enjoy!

Chapter 1:

Understanding Technical Analysis

When it comes to ensuring that your successful trade percentage only increases as time goes on, you may find it useful to branch out of analyzing the fundamentals of a company to determine if its stock is worth considering and to also analyze it technically. Technical analysis studies past market trends with the goal of accurately predicting those that are likely to occur again in the future. Technical analysis is ideal for those that like the idea of determining future performance by looking at previous prices, without having to dig through mountains of paperwork to find the details you are looking for. While the past will never be able to truly predict the future 100 percent of the time, technical analysis is useful when combined with a basic understanding of market mentality for generating predictions that are accurate within reason.

Price charts: A price chart is one of the most basic tools of technical analysis, as the name implies, it charts the price movement of a particular underlying asset along the x axis and the timeframe along the y axis. There are numerous different types of charts to choose from, of course, and many of them are briefly touched on here. If you are just getting the hang of technical analysis, however, then you will want to focus on the easier charts such as the bar chart, the candlestick chart, the point and click chart and the line chart.

Line chart: The line chart is the most basic chart that most traders start with as all it does is show a list of closing prices over a specific period of time. The lines are formed after the day's grouping of closing prices has been determined and they are then connected with the ultimate goal of determining the current trend that is influencing the stock in question. This means you won't be able to find other details including things like the opening price for the given period, or the overall results for a given day, but you will be able to determine if the day is positive or negative, often without much of the noise that surrounds other charts which makes it a useful first stop when looking into the details behind a stock you are unfamiliar with.

Bar chart: A bar chart provides additional detail when compared to a line chart by adding in other aspects of the stock's performance for the day. The top and bottom of the bar represent the high and the low for the day respectively while the price at closing is indicated on the ride side of the bar with the help of a handy dash. The dash on the left side of the bar shows the starting price. and if the stock increased in value for the day then the bar will be black while it will either be red or clear if the price decreased throughout the day.

Candlestick chart: A candlestick is similar to a bar chart in many ways, though it also provides additional relevant information that is more detailed overall. It includes the range for the day, expressed as a line, as with a bar graph, but when you view a candlestick chart you will also notice a wide bar near the vertical line which indicates the degree of difference the price experienced over a given period of time. If the price increases for the day, then the candlestick will not be shaded in and if the price decreased throughout the day then it will typically be shaded in red as well.

Point and figure chart: While less used than the charts discussed above, the point and figure chart has been around for more than 100 years and can still prove as useful today as when it first gained popularity. This chart is useful if you need to determine how the price is likely to move, without taking volume or timing into account. As such, it is purely an indicator of price with any and all outside noise completely muted which means you can guarantee the results won't be skewed in one direction or another.

A point and figure chart can be easily picked out from the crowd as it is made up of Xs and Os rather than lines and points. The Xs will indicate points where positive trends occurred while the Os will indicate periods of downward movement. You will also notice numbers and letters listed along the bottom of the chart which correspond to months as well as dates. This type of chart will also make it clear how much the price is going to have to move in order for an X to become an O or an O to become an X.

Understanding trend and range

In order to profit from the use of technical analysis, one of the first things you will need to determine about your trading style is if you are going to be focusing on trading via range or trading based on trends. While they are both related to price, the two are going to come together very differently in practice which means you are going to want to focus on one or the other if you are going to be successful when using technical analysis.

If you are interested in trades that go with the flow, then you may be more comfortable trading on trend as it helps you determine what a majority of the market is currently up to. You goal in these scenarios will be to decide which trends are the most likely to manifest themselves in the future so that you have the full amount of time to jump on them for yourself and reap the greatest amounts of profits possible. If you are considering this type of trading, then you will want to generally stick to smaller trades as it can be risky and anticipated trends can fail to materialize in the way you might have thought they would. Trading via trend is ideal for those who prefer high risk and the greater potential for reward it brings along with it.

Range trading, on the other hand, is better suited for those who are willing to forgo some amount of profit for more reliable returns. The range in question is going to be the price that a given stock is going to return to twice or more throughout the time you are holding it, allowing you to profit each time. The market is going to present you with different challenges every single day in the form of different trends and potential opportunities. Despite the fact that the movement may seem to operate in completely random patterns, there are always ways to tell its true intentions, if you have figured out where to look, as to the direction it is most likely to take. The opening range approach is one that professionals have been using for decades as a way to start off with an idea of the market's moods to make any potential forthcoming profits even easier to attain.

When using the opening range as a starting point, you can then locate the truth of the current market that will indicate if the bears or the bulls are going to be in charge for the day. In order to use it effectively, it is important to understand that the opening range high and low levels will be of critical importance when it comes to levels of resistance and support throughout the day. Understanding this fact will let you anticipate the levels where the market is more likely to accelerate or reverse and lead to big moves in the long run. Looking at the trading day through this lens means you are more likely to be able to make the right moves in the right market and anticipate future swings instead of watching them pass you by.

You don't need to find the perfect entry point in this instance, you simply need to get in at a point where you will be in on the ground floor the next time the cycle repeats itself. Range trading can take more time to get working properly, however, so it is best to have a larger bankroll when aiming to successfully put it into effect.

Getting started successfully

When using technical analysis. it is important to always keep in mind the fact that it functions based on the core belief that the way the price of a given stock is going to fluctuate in the future is going to be directly connected to the patterns its price has followed in the past. As such, it doesn't matter which market you chose to focus on primarily, you will always find that there is more technical data out there than you will ever be able to parse successfully. Luckily, you won't have to sort through this mass of data by yourself, you will have plenty of technical tools at your disposal including indicators, charts, trends and more to help ensure you find the success you seek with as few speedbumps along the way as possible.

While some of the methods you will be asked to apply might seem arcane at first, the fact of the matter is that all you are essentially doing is looking to determine future trends along with their relative strengths. This, in turn, is crucial to your long-term success and will make each of your trades more reliable practically every single time.

Understand core assumptions: Technical analysis is all about measuring the relative value of a particular trade or underlying asset by using available tools to find otherwise invisible patterns that, ideally, few other people have currently noticed. When it comes to using technical analysis properly you are going to always need to assume three things are true. First and foremost, the market ultimately discounts everything; second, trends will always be an adequate predictor of price and third, history is bound to repeat itself when given enough time to do so.

Technical analysis believes that the current price of a specific underlying asset is the only true metric that matters when it comes to considering the current state of tings both in the market and outside it. This is due to the fact that everything else about the market has already been factored through the price to get it to where it is now which means that analyzing it, when compared to the overall state of the market should provide you all of the information you need.

Additionally, technical analysis holds to be true the fact that the current value of an underlying asset moves based on the trend that has been established, which means it can be tracked as long as you know what to look for. What this means is that once a trend has been identified then it is really just a matter of waiting for it to come around again before you can take advantage of it. Statistically speaking, it is always more likely that a trend is going to repeat than a new trend is going to form out of nowhere or a trend is going to reverse dramatically instead.

This idea, then, is key to the technical analysis assumption that history is bound to repeat itself sooner or later as far as market price is concerned. This is not just a saying, it is a summation of an unavoidable fact of human nature, specifically, humans like patterns. As such, if a certain pattern can be perceived in a series of data you can expect people to find it, and once they have, they are likely to respond to it in the same way as well. This is what makes common technical analysis patterns so useful, despite the fact that some of them were first discovered more than 100 years ago. This just goes to show that public opinion and action in relation to price changes is always going to be the same no matter what.

All about trend: Being aware of trend and how it can affect the ways you will analyze a specific trade is key to your long-term success through technical analysis. When on the lookout for trend, it can be any clear direction that the price of a given stock is taking that is clear enough to cut through all of the noise that naturally infects the market as a whole. Trends can be either strong enough to see from a mile away or weak enough to easily miss even if you are looking for them. Essentially it just means that just because a given trend isn't immediately visible then this doesn't mean it isn't there. Likewise, you are going to always want to ensure that the trend you think you are following is really there as it can be easy to misinterpret false data if you aren't careful.

The easiest way to ensure you are on the right track when it comes to these types of trends is to focus purely on the highs and lows and leave everything else where it is and ignore it as market noise. Even still, your results don't need to be all or nothing, instead you are going to want to keep an eye out for a clear pattern that increases or decreases over time with either lower highs or higher lows. Positive trends are referred to as uptrends and negative trends are known as reversals. Somewhere in the middle are horizontal trends which have roughly equal numbers of highs and lows balancing them out.

When you tap into specific trends that appear to be long lasting then you can realistically expect that the next round the trend experiences to last even longer, though you will want to avoid giving it free reign until the trend starts to head back in the other direction and thus become more manageable as a result. If you find yourself staring at a short trend, then you will want to ensure that you aren't just focusing on a small part of a bigger trend that you aren't quite aware of yet. To make this process even easier you will want to spread your shorter charts out to longer timeframes to ensure you aren't accidentally missing the forests for the trees.

While this can make the overall process much more cumbersome, it can prevent you from making a huge mistake without even realizing it. By contrast, if you are having trouble homing in on a shorter trend then daily or even minute-based charts can make that process easier.

Mapping visible trends: Once you have locked in on a trend you are curious in finding out more about, the next thing you will want to do is create a trendline that allow you to map out all of the details you've found. This can be accomplished by simply drawing a straight line through the data points to make the trend more visible. If the trend is positive, then you will want to connect the dots of the various lows that are being measured while if it is a negative trend you will want to connect the relevant highs. This line is what is known as the resistance line and it represents the market's natural inclination to push back once prices hit a point that is either significantly above or significantly below the average. This doesn't indicate the likelihood of the next price movement, just its overall limits.

Once you have created the initial line, you will then want to create an additional pair of lines, one for the support level and one for the resistance level. The support line will connect all of the lows while the resistance lines will connect all of the highs. The resulting channel that you then create will likely be either positive or negative though neutral channels representing sideways movement are also possible. Regardless, the channel you create needs to continue for a long enough time to show where the price breaks away from the status quo. This moment is going to represent your ideal entry point that will give you the best chance see the greatest overall return on your investment.

Chapter 2:

Fundamental Analysis Primer

While this book will primarily concern itself with technical analysis, principles, technical analysis and fundamental analysis often go hand in hand so a discussion of one would be incomplete without the other.

When it comes to determining which stocks, and therefore which companies, are going to be the most likely to continue to produce dividends in the long run, one of the best ways to go about doing so is through the process of fundamental analysis. Fundamental analysis is a technique that works to determine the underlying value of a given security through a focus on the things that affect a company's future prospects as well as its day to day business. It also works on the economy as a whole or on specific industries, depending on where you want to start. At its most basic, it simply refers to the analysis of the economic well-being of a company instead of simply looking at the movements of its stock price.

Fundamental analysis answers a host of differing questions including:

- Is the company being straightforward about its profits?
- Is it able to reliably pay its debts?
- Is it currently turning a profit?
- Is it strong enough to continue being profitable in the long-term?
- Is its revenue moving in the right direction?

While these can be extremely involved questions, they all essentially boil down to the decision of whether or not a company is a good investment and if they are likely to continue producing dividends in the long-term. Fundamental analysis can also be thought of as a type of toolbox that can make answering this question much easier.

Quantitative and Qualitative analysis

Fundamental analysis is all about researching the fundamentals of a given company, but that alone won't be enough to tell you what you need to know unless you know what fundamentals you are working with to start. Unfortunately, this can be more comprehensive than you might hope as the fundamentals can include practically anything that affects the economic viability of your chosen company in one way or another. Basic fundamentals include things such as profit or revenue, but they can also include things like the quality of its leadership and its market share.

Generally speaking, different fundamental factors can be classified in two ways, quantitative and qualitative. Quantitative factors are those that are purely numerical in nature, things that will be written down and discussed during the next investors' meeting. Qualitative factors are those that focus more on the inherent qualities of the company and the things that make it great, which naturally makes them more difficult to track. Qualitative factors are generally less tangible and include things like its name recognition, the patents it holds and the quality of its board members.

Neither of these types of factors are going to naturally be superior to the together, and they will typically provide better results when they are used in conjunction with one another. For example, consider the Coca-Cola Company. For quantitative factors, an analyst could look at its P/E ratio, earnings per share and, of course, its annual dividend payout rate. For qualitative factors you would need to consider its overall brand recognition which takes it from a company that essentially sells carbonated sugar water to a company that is recognized by almost everyone on the planet. While this figure can't be quantified with a dollar amount it is, without a doubt, one of the major contributing factors to its overall success.

Qualitative analysis

Qualitative factors are generally less tangible and include things like its name recognition, the patents it holds and the quality of its board members. Qualitative factors to consider include

Business model: The first thing that you are going to want to do when you catch wind of a company that might be worth following up on is to check out its business model which is more or less a generalization of how it makes its money. You can typically find these sorts of details on the company website or in its 10-K filing.

Competitive advantage: It is also important to consider the various competitive advantages that the company you have your eye on might have over its competition. Companies that are going to be successful in the long-term are always going to have an advantage over their competition in one of two ways. They can either have better operational effectiveness or improved strategic positioning. Operational effectiveness is the name given to doing the same things as the competition but in a more efficient and effective way. Strategic positioning occurs when a company gains an edge by doing things that nobody else is doing.

Leadership: The type of management that is currently leading a company is going to go a long way towards determining if it is going to be successful in the long run. After all, even the most well thought out business plan will fail if it isn't able to rely on the right infrastructure to support it in the long run. When it comes to analyzing management, the first place you are going to want to look is the corporate information section of the company's website. This won't provide you with much more than the names of the folks at the top, but if they have been around the block, then names should be enough to pull up everything you need to know about their past work experiences. While this might not ultimately amount to much, if there is something unfortunate in their past this should bring it to light.

Quantitative analysis

The extreme volume of data, coupled with the great degree of variance between the truth and reality that can easily be found in the average company's financial statement means it can be intimidating to roll up your sleeves and get your hands dirty. This is just what you will have to do with quantitative analysis, however, and once you get the hang of it you will find the average financial statement is a goldmine of useful information when it comes to determining if a specific company is going to be a good investment moving forward. Unlike with qualitative points of interest, qualitative concepts are all cold, hard facts that are not open for interpretation.

Balance sheet: The balance sheet for a specific company is going to show everything that has to do with the company's assets for a set period of time as well as their liabilities and their assets. The balance sheet is also going to show how the company's financial structure is divided by dividing the company's equity by the combination of shareholders and liabilities in order to determine its current assets.

In this scenario specifically, the assets in question are going to represent various resources that the company is actively participating in at a given point and time. It will also include things such as machinery, property, cash and inventory. It will also show the total value of any financing that has been used up to this point in order to generate those resources. Financing can come from either liabilities or equity. Liabilities include debt that needs to be repaid while equity includes money that the owners or other investors have put into the business. This can even include profits from previous years which are then known as retained earnings.

Income statement: If the balance sheet is the snapshot of the company's fundamentals, the income statement is a closeup of how the company is performing over a specific space of time. The most commonly used income statement is going to be either quarterly or annually, depending on the company in question. Income statements provide details on expenses, profits and revenues that resulted from the business that took place over the specified period of time.

Cash flow statement: A cashflow statement shows the complete record of any and all cash that is both coming into and going out of the company over a set period of time. The cash flow statement focuses on a number of specific activities including:

- Operating cash flow which is cash that is generated by business operations that take place each day.

- Cash from investing which is generally used to invest in assets along with profits that may have been generated through the sale of long-term assets such as equipment or the sale of another business that was previously owned by the company.

- Cash due to financing is money that is received or paid off based on borrowing or issuing funds.

The cashflow statement is particularly important as it is more difficult for business to manipulate it than some of the other financial documents listed. While it could be possible for accountants to get tricky with earnings, it is much more difficult to fake the amount of funds on hand in the bank. As such, many investors consider the cashflow statement to be the most reliable metric for a given company's performance.

Finding the details: While tracking down all the disparate financial statements on the company's you are considering purchasing stock in can be cumbersome, the Securities and Exchange Commission (SEC) requires all publicly traded companies to submit regular filings outlining all of their financial activities including a variety of different financial statements. This also includes information such as managerial discussions, reports from auditors, deep dives into the operations and prospects of upcoming years and more.

These types of details can all be found in the 10-K filing that each company is required to file every year, along with the 10-Q filing that they must send out once per quarter. Both types of documents can be found online, both at the corporate website for the company as well as on the SEC website. As the version that hits the corporate site doesn't need to be complete, it is best to visit SEC.gov and get to know the Electronic Data Gathering, Analysis and Retrieval system (EDGAR) which automates the process of indexing, validating, collecting, forward and accepting submissions. As this system was designed in the mid-90s, however, it is important to dedicate some time to learning the process as it is more cumbersome than 20 years of user interface advancements have lead you to expect.

Chapter 3:

Technical Indicators to Watch

It can be difficult for many traders, especially those who are just getting used to technical analysis, to see the somewhat hidden signs that are pointing towards buy or sell that are often sitting right in front of them, which can lead to them sitting on the sidelines while profitable trades pass them by. What these types of traders are failing to understand is that there is no one right way to trade which means you are going to need to consider several different types of technical indicators if you hope to use technical analysis to bring in the profits you have always dreamed of. While there are countless types of technical indicators that you could consider, the following are the ones you should get familiar with first, before expanding your horizons as desired from there.

In order to make the most of the effort, however, it is important to have a clear understanding of the benefits of the technical indicators you are looking for as well as their strengths and weaknesses. Broadly speaking, technical indicators are any one of a variety of different metrics with a value that is directly tied to the current price of a specific underlying asset. The goal of all technical indicators, then, is to show the direction the price of an underlying asset is going to move as well as what the extent of that movement is likely going to be. This is done through a mixture of analyzing past patterns and determining how and when they are going to repeat themselves in the future.

Luckily, technical indicators can be extremely easy to spot once you know what to look for as they do not inherently analyze any of the fundamentals discussed in the previous chapter and instead are focused completely on price movement. They are especially useful in the short-term and end up losing some of their usefulness in the long-term as they often lack the breadth of data that would be required to make them particularly useful in long-term concerns. As such, long term investors are typically known to use technical indicators as a way of determining the right entry points to take advantage of and the right exit points to have in place to prevent financial disaster.

Find a way to follow trends

While advanced traders often find success when it comes to trading against the prevailing trends of the market, it is much easier for novice traders to go with the flow and make the same types of trades as a majority of the market. This can also be easier said than done, however, especially if you don't have a ready means of determining which trends are going to pop up where. While some people will swear that a trend following tool is really all you need to get started trading successfully, in reality, they are only really helpful when it comes to helping you to determine if the right choice in the current market is to enter into a long position or if a short position is a better choice. One of the easiest, and as a result most reliable, trend measuring tools to use is what is generally referred to as the moving average crossover.

Crossover: The crossover is the point on the chart where a specific underlying asset that you are tracking and the indicator that you are used to tracking it intersect with one another. Taking this one step further, the moving average crossover is an easy way for traders to determine when a change to the current trend is likely forthcoming. A moving average is a technical indicator that makes it easier for traders to smooth out the price movement of a given underlying asset. It is considered a type of lagging indicator as it will only every function to show you where the price has been, not where it's going.

Simple moving average: The simple moving average has a bit more going on than the traditional moving average as it calculates the price of the specific underlying asset over numerous different timeframes before dividing the total by the number of time periods that are being used in the process. When using this process, it is common for successful traders to keep an eye out for averages in the short-term to cross the point that is greater than the existing average over an extended period of time which is a good sign that an uptrend is incoming. It is also possible for the short-term averages to generate types of support in case the price sees an unexpected pullback.

Simple moving averages are also especially useful as they can be easily customized based on the number of timeframes you are interested in pursing as well as the number that will do the most good in the moment. The goal of this process is then to minimize the overall influence of volatility on the trade, something that traders of all types are always going to be interested in for one reason or another. The greater the moving average's timeframe, the more regulated the simple moving average is going to be and the shorter the timeframe, the more volatile the average is going to be.

Moving averages are important to consider when it comes to finding pricing trends with the real potential to shake an existing trend out of its rut in the marketplace. It can prove useful in scenarios where you need to identify the overall trend the underlying asset is experiencing with only a few additional calculations. Even better, you can add in a second simple moving average to cover the different timeframes and find even more impressive trends as a result.

Find a way to confirm existing trends

After you have a clear idea as to how to determine if the underlying assets you are considering are currently part of a positive or negative trend, then you will need to consider a technical indicator that will make it easier for you to confirm that the trend you are looking at is going to prove to be as useful as you may have initially hoped. This type of indicator is especially useful as the trends that are uncovered via the simple moving average are often prone to extreme periods of sporadic movement that can be difficult to compensate for, even if you know it is coming. As such, a secondary tool for trend confirmation can be useful to ensure that you don't waste time on trends that are not ultimately going to pan out.

The purpose of this tool is not to then generate buy or sell signals related to a given underlying assets but to instead to agree or disagree with the trend-following tool you decide to use. As such, when both the tools result in a confirmed bullish market then you can feel more confident when you choose a long trade related to the underlying assets you are curious in learning more about. The same goes for a doubly confirmed bearish market and short selling the pair that you have chosen. The most commonly used confirmation tool is one that is referred to as the moving average convergence divergence or MACD for short. This tool measures the amount of difference that there is between two averages that have been smoothed to minimize ancillary noise.

The difference between the two results is then further smoothed by the process before then being matched against the moving average that it relates to as well. If the resulting smoothed average is still greater than the existing moving average, then you can be sure that the positive trend you were chasing actually exists. Meanwhile, if the smoothed average ends up below the existing moving average than any negative trends will be confirmed instead.

MACD Moving average convergence divergence: When it comes to confirming a trend that you have noticed, MACD is the choice of professional traders everywhere. When utilized properly it measures the difference of two averages that have already been smoothed out to minimize random noise. If this average ends up being greater than the moving average, then the trend is positive while if it is less the trend is negative. The value of the MACD indicator will be 0 at the point where the averages intersect. The direction at which they cross should correlate to the trend that you uncover.

To utilize MACD properly you need to first determine a longer and a shorter moving average. With this done, MACD works by taking into account the value left over by subtracting the longer from the shorter before then plotting the results out over between 12 and 26 days. If the two averages line up with the shorter above the longer then you know that momentum is increasing while the opposite is also true. This situation shows that you should hold off on any trades as the situation is likely going to improve sooner than later.

When plotting out the MACD you will also want to plot a moving average at the same time as this will help you understand when the momentum is likely to shift. Plotting the moving average of the MACD is known as the signal line and it is an option in most trading platforms. When the MACD line crosses at a point above the signal line then the trend is bullish and if it crosses below then it is bearish. If the results are bullish then this is a strong indicator that the trend is soon going to reverse.

While this tool can be useful if you are curious about the short-term direction the underlying assets you favor are going to move, it has its limitations as well. Specifically, it can generate mixed signals if the market is in a state of high volatility as numerous small movements tend to generate false signals. Additionally, as a lagging indicator it can generate numerous different signals if the period of time you are tracking is exceedingly long. Finally, it is important to keep in mind that it is largely useless when it comes to comparing underlying assets that are sitting at different price points. Remember, it is useful for comparing a pair of moving averages, not for comparing assets directly.

When it comes to plotting the MACD line, it is important to always plot a moving average as well to ensure you have a clear line that indicates when the momentum is likely to shift. This line is known as either the trigger line or the signal line and it is created by finding the moving average of the MACD specifically. This line can be plotted automatically via most trading programs so that it shows up next to the relevant charts. If the MACD line crosses above the signal line, then it is clear that things are bearish while if it crosses below the signal line then the trend is bullish instead.

In order to successfully make a profit with a bullish MACD, you will need to have a very clear idea of what the optimum sell value is going to be as this portion of the market is still considered advisable to sell according to the moving average. When a bullish crossover occurs it typically indicates the onset of a reversal though it is still riskier to go through with such a trade than when the MACD is greater than zero.

The short-term moving average is general determined based on the 12-day EMA while a longer moving average is typically based on the 26-day EMA. Assuming this is the case, you can assume the value of the MACD indicator is going to equal zero at the point where the two EMAs meet. The direction at which the cross-through occurs at the zero-line will determine the direction the trend is likely to continue moving in for the near future along with details you can use relating to its momentum as well.

Relative strength index: The relative strength index (RSI) is useful when it comes to determining the current level of risk surrounding a given trade. When used properly it will allow you to determine the entry point with the least amount of risk. Essentially it will allow you to determine if an existing trend is moving in a bullish direction, thus allowing you to determine if buying into the position is a strong move.

If you do decide to jump in as soon as a new position is established, you will likely need to pace your first trade as soon as the trend is discovered, which has the potential to lead to significant gains if the trend continues as expected, while also having the potential to lead to loss if the trend reverses in a way you did not expect. The other choice, then, is to wait for the trend to become more thoroughly confirmed, while giving up some of the profit along with some of the risk. Regardless of which you chose, you are going to want to consider an indicator that determines if the underlying asset in question is going to see more movement or if it is likely all tapped out when it comes to additional people to sell and or buy.

While there are several different types of indicators out there that fill this particular roll, the RSI is the tool that is used most frequently. It is often used to calculate results in increments of three days and measures the total sum of positive days and negative days before calculating a value with a range between 0 and 100. If the movement of the underlying asset in this period is generally positive, then the indicator will end up closer to 100 and if the movement is negative the result will be closer to 0. As such, if the result is close to 50 then the results are considered to be neutral.

RSIs are particularly useful when used to monitor oscillating indicators which tend to vary between differing values at the extreme ends, each representing a scenario where the underlying asset in question is either under bought or under sold respectively. The RSI will allow you to determine which condition is currently in play as well as any remaining potential that you turn a profit.

To determine the RSI, you use the following formula: 100/1+RS where RSI=100- and RS is equal to the average of the close on the days that saw an overall positive underlying asset movement divided by the average of the close on the days that saw an overall negative underlying asset movement. Typically, the indicator of a position that is overbought is 70 or higher, while the indicator of a position that is oversold is 30 or below. These can be reset to 80 and 20 respectively, if you tend to have a higher tolerance for trading risk.

If you are typically interested on entering once pullback on the price has occurred the you may find that you are interested in taking a long position if you see that the 50-day average is moving higher than the 200-day average while the RSI is dropping. Alternatively, if you are in a position where you see the 50-day drop below the 200-day while the RSI is rising, then you are likely going to want to take a short position related to the underlying assets in question.

When it comes to ensuring you are using the RSI as effectively as possible, many traders find that it is best to compare the results they find to those found through the use of the moving average crossovers that can be applied in the short-term. This goes for both the moving average in the 2-day and the 10-day timeframe as both can provide you with the points of crossover you are looking for to determine the likelihood that the price is going to reverse in the near future. These crossovers are likely to coincide with either the 70/30 or 80/20 spit that you established with your RSI. It can also easily be used in conjunction with any momentum-based indicators you are using in order to provide a superior means of determining both entry and exit points.

3-day RSI: The 3-day RSI is worth considering in addition to the standard RSI as it will often show you how to maximize your profit while still keeping your risk to acceptable levels, whatever it is they may be. If you are holding a long position, then once you see an RSI of greater than 70 you can safely assume that it is a good idea to take half of your profits while at the same time setting an exit point that is half again as high for the remainder of your holdings. The same tactic is recommended on a short position with an RSI of 30.

Trailing stop: The trailing stop is another useful indicator when it comes to determining potential profit. It allows you to easily set exit points that allow for your potential profits to grow, without leaving them open for the extra risk that would allow them to grow unchecked. The trailing stop is a flexible version of the traditional stop that automatically tracks the movement of the underlying asset in question to ensure it does not need to be reset if there is a sudden, short burst of movement. As with all stop orders, a trailing stop helps newer traders to keep emotion out of the equation by selling based on predetermined conditions.

Rather than being based on specific prices, the trailing stop works based on the amount of movement the underlying asset experienced instead. As an example, if you decided to set a trailing loss that was set to trigger at a 30 percent decrease in value then short fits and starts won't be enough to move it unless it drops 30 percent at one time.

Chapter 4:

Understanding Candlestick Charts

Candlestick basics

Candlestick trading starts with a price bar, which is a visual representation of the movement that a particular stock has taken over a preset amount of time that can be either weekly, daily, hourly, every 30 minutes or every 5 minutes.

When it comes to creating a price bar that is truly accurate you will want to collect a few different pieces of information. First you will want to consider the price the stock in question started the day at, the next is the amount that it peaked at, you will also want to know its overall low point, and finally, the closing price. When you plug this information into the platform that you are using you will see that the data is ultimately plotted so that it looks like a box that has been struck through with a line. The points of that line equate to the low and high price while the outer bottom and uppermost edges of the box signify the closing as well as the opening price. Stocks that ended higher than they started are colored in one color and stocks that ended lower than they started are then colored in using a separate color.

Candlestick formation: This box that has been created is commonly called a candlestick and it does more than just provide you with details of what has happened in the past, it can also make it easier for you to determine what is likely going to happen in the future.

Range: The range of the candlestick is the visual representation of the current level of volatility the market is experiencing. The greater the current volatility level, the less reliable you can expect your chosen underlying assets to be when compared to their historical averages. You can then determine the volatility of the market by looking to the size of the line in relation to the overall size of the box. If the volatility is currently high, the box will be large, and the line will be relatively small. If the current volatility is low, the opposite will be the case.

Body: The body of the candle relates to the physical orientation of the box as it relates to either the opening or the closing price. If the price closes higher than it opened, you can assume the market improved overall, while the reverse will also be true. It is also important to take note of the size of the box as a whole as the greater the size of the box, the stronger the market likely is overall. If the box is so large that you can't see any bar at all, then you will know that the market is likely in a period of neutral flux.

Split line: After you have a clear handle on the body and the range, you will then be ready to move on to the top half of the line. This line portion caps at the highpoint for the price for the day while also indicating the point where supply started to exceed demand once more, leading to a decreasing price overall. This also means that the top point of the line can also be seen as the maximum amount of pressure that the underlying stock experienced in the time period. The lower half of the bar details the same specifics except regarding the low for the day and the point demand began to exceed supply.

Two price bars: If you decide to add a second price bar to the analysis that you are doing you will be able to use the pair as a set of cornerstones giving you a decent idea of what the price is doing outside of the vacuum of a single bar. The second bar allows you to determine if what you saw from the first bar was simply a fluke or was actually something that is actionable enough to move on in real time. In time, you will likely find this exceptionally useful if you need to determine if a bar is actually wide or is in fact average or other forms of comparison as well. This will allow you to understand the price action in a way that is more specific, and thus more effective, than it would often otherwise be.

Candlestick strategies

Signals: First and foremost, you are only going to want to target stocks that are strongly trending in one direction. Second, the low (downtrend) or high (uptrend) bar needs to occur in the middle of a candlestick. Finally, the final bar needs to close either above the high of the first two candlesticks. With this standard in place it will then be painfully obvious once a given trend has reversed.

This strategy works in a variety of timeframes. As an example, assume you are working off of the 5-minute chart before detecting a stock that hit its low and then sharply reversed upwards. The third bar in the series would then close at a point that is higher than the highs of both of the other bars. While you can move forward if the close is above the high of the middle candlestick, it is better to know what the third candle is doing for added insurance.

The exit strategy for this pattern is just a simple moving average or even a price target. Just be sure you watch it closely and you should be fine. A good rule of thumb with this pattern is a 3 to 1 risk and reward ratio for the trade. Additionally, it is important to keep in mind that this strategy can generate quick returns no matter what time of day it is and in any market type.

These days, more and more day traders are trying to fake one another out when it comes to specific trades. Unfortunately, the 3-bar reversal pattern is not immune to this problem. One of the main reasons that the 3-bar reversal pattern fails is when volatility isn't high enough. If the market is exceedingly choppy, then the formation you are looking for is really going to be nothing more than a pause in the overall action.

This means it will not ultimately result in the type upswing or downswing that you are looking for. Adding in additional methods of confirmation before you choose your entry point will make it easier to avoid these false signals.

If you buy into this type of trend it is important to be aware that it isn't moving as you would like and cut your losses before they get worse. The sooner you bail, the sooner you can get back to looking for a reversal that is actually profitable.

Hook reversal: A hook reversal is a type of candlestick pattern that can generally only be found in the shorter timeframe charts. They can appear during positive and negative trends and are useful when it comes to finding out about a new trend that will mark the reversal of the current trend. This type of pattern is known to appear with a higher low as well as a lower high when compared to the candlestick of the previous day. You can tell this pattern from the rest because the size difference between the body of the first and second bar is quite small when compared to other, similar patterns.

If this type of pattern materializes around a positive trend, then the open will often be near the previous high while the low will be close to the relevant low. This pattern is also often typically associated with other more common positions because the second candle body often forms within the body of the first candle. The relative strength for this signal will be tied directly to the overall strength of the trend. The stronger the trend, the stronger the signal that this pattern will give off.

Abandoned baby: This candlestick pattern can prove especially useful when it comes to determining points where a reversal might start within the current trend. This type of pattern is created from a trio of candlesticks with several distinctive characteristics. The first bar is going to be a red candlestick that is large and visible within a previously defined downtrend. The second bar will have an open equal to its close that gaps beneath the close of the first bar.

The final bar is going to be a white candlestick that is large and opens higher than the second bar. This bar also represents changing trader sentiment. This is a fairly uncommon pattern, but it can be used reliably if you are looking to predict a change to an existing downtrend. The accuracy of the signal will then be further enhanced when combined with additional technical indicators such as the MACD and RSI.

The bearish abandoned baby is useful if you are curious if an existing positive trend is likely going to reverse sooner than later. It is also a type of trio pattern and the first portion is the white candlestick that is found within the current positive trend. The second bar will be the same as that in the middle of the bullish abandoned baby and the final bar will be a large red candle that will open somewhere below the second bar.

Outside reversal: This is a price chart pattern that can be visible when the low and high for the day both exceed the high of the trading session of the previous day. This pattern is referred to as a bearish engulfing pattern if the second bar is a down candlestick and a bullish engulfing pattern if the second bar is instead an up candlestick. This pattern typically proves useful if you need to identify future price movement as well as determine if it is going to be positive or negative. It typically occurs at the point where the first price bar drops outside the range of the previous price bar when its high is above the previous high and the low is as well. As a general rule, if the outside reversal occurs at the level of resistance then the signal is bearish and if it occurs at the support level then it is bullish.

Chapter 5:

Consolidation Patterns to Watch

Consolidation is the term used in technical analysis as a means of describing the tendency of price to stick to a previously defined pattern across multiple trading levels. Generally speaking, consolidation can be thought of as a period of indecisiveness that comes to an end once the price moves outside this predetermined pattern. These types of consolidation are surprisingly common and can be found across any price chart at virtually any time frame. When they do appear, it is the goal of technical traders to use them when it comes to finding support and resistance levels so that informed buying and selling decisions will be made.

These support or resistance levels are generated by an underlying asset's natural propensity to vary over a specific period of time. As such, once the price moves beyond either the pre-existing levels of resistance or support, volatility will increase dramatically as a result. This period of volatility is when smart traders jump in to make serious profits in a very short period of time. Additionally, many technical traders believe that if the breakout occurs in favor of resistance then the price in question is typically going to continue moving upward which means you would naturally want to go long in response. If the breakout occurs on par with the support, however, then the odds are strong that the price will decrease as a result which means you would need to utilize a short position to take full advantage of it.

Pennants and flags: Both pennants and flags are signs of retracements, or deviations from the existing trend that become visible in the short-term when viewed in relation to the primary trend. Retracements typically result in no breakout occurring from either the support or resistance levels, but this ultimately won't matter as much as the fact that the underlying asset won't be following the dominant trend to begin with. The absence of a breakout will result in the trend being relative short overall. The resistance and support lines of the pennant occur within a larger trend before converging in a point. A flag is much the same except that the support and resistance lines form parallel instead.

Pennants and flags are both more likely to be found in the mid-section portion of the primary trend. They typically last as long as two weeks before returning to the primary trend line. They tend to be most frequently associated with falling volume which means that if you notice a pennant or flag with volume that isn't falling then you are likely actually looking at a reversal.

Head Above Shoulders Formation: If you are looking for indicators of how long any one particular trend is likely to continue, then looking for a grouping of three peaks in a price chart, known as the head above shoulders formation, can indicate a bearish pattern moving forward. The peaks to the left and to the right of the primary peak, also known as the shoulders, should be somewhat smaller than the head peak and also connect at a specific price. This price is known as the neckline and when it reaches the right shoulder the price will likely then plunge noticeably. This formation typically occurs when a large group of traders is holding out for one last price increase after a long run of price gains for a specific security. When this occurs but the trend then changes, and the prices fall then the head above shoulders will appear. If you see the opposite, that is an inverse head above shoulders, then you know that the security holding this pattern is actually likely to soon increase in price.

Cup and Handle: The cup and handle formation tends to appear most frequently when an underlying asset reaches a peak price before falling sharply for the majority of a single trading period or more. The security will rebound eventually which will show that the time is right to buy. This indicator also shows that a specific trend is on the rise which means you will want to take advantage of any of these types of formations that you see while you can.

The handle forms on the cup when those who bought into the underlying asset at a preceding high point get tired of waiting and start to sell which, in turn, gives new investors a likely point to buy in. This type of formation is often slow to form and can take a year or more to become fully visible in some cases. The best time to take advantage of this type of trend is when the handle is just starting to form. If you see the cup form without the handle, then you will want to consider any day to day patterns that are forming as they will give you a strong indicator as to the likely effectiveness of buying in at a specific point.

Gann Indicators: While derided by some, Gann indicators have been used by day traders for decades, through many significant changes in the market, and remain a useful way of determining the direction an asset is likely to move in next. Gann angles are used to measure certain relevant elements including time, price and pattern which help the trader determine the past, present and future of the market and how that information will determine the future of the price.

While often assumed to be functionally similar to trend lines, in reality, Gann angles are quite different though they can be created automatically through many trading programs. They are diagonal lines which move at a fixed rate.

If you compare a Gann angle to a trend line, then you will see that it makes it much easier to predict the likely movement of the price at a fixed point in the future. This is not to say that it will always be accurate, but it can be useful when it comes to determining the location and relevant strength of a particular trend. As all times exist on the same line, the Gann angle can then also be used to predict resistance, direction strength and support as well as the timing on tops and bottoms.

Gann angles are most commonly used to determine the likely resistance and support as it only requires the trade to determine the right scale of the chart and then draw in the 1x2, 1x1 and 2x1 Gann angles from the primary bottoms to the tops. This makes it less complicated for the trader to frame the market, thus making it easier to determine the way the market is moving based on this predetermined framework. Positive trend angles indicate support in the market while negative trend angles indicate resistance. By understanding the angle on the chart, traders can more easily determine the most profitable times to buy and sell.

Additionally, it is important to always keep in mind the many ways that the market can move between various angles. If the market breaks from a single angle then it will likely move on towards the next, making your job to determine where it is likely headed next. Support and resistance can also be found by combining the angles along with the horizontal lines. If you find that lots of angles appear to be clustering together near a specific price point, especially on a long-term chart, then you should be able to assume the resistance and support in that area is worth a closer look.

As previously mentioned, the most important Gann angles are those that are 2x1, 1x1 and 1x2. The 1x2 angle indicates that one unit of price moves for every two units of time, the 1x1 indicates that price and time move at the same rate and 2x1 indicates that two price units moves for every single unit of time. Additional angles can be extrapolated following the same formula including 8x1, 4x1, 1x4 and 1x8. When it comes to performing this type of analysis it is important to always use the proper scale which is a square chart whereby the 1x1 angle moves at an angle of 45 degrees. This is a test then as only when the chart is scaled properly will the angle appear appropriately.

In addition to resistance and support, these angles also provide a valid indicator as to the strength of the market. If the 1x1 angle is relatively close to the trading trend, then this indicates the market is balanced. If it is near the 1x2 angle, then the trend is weaker than the possible 1x1 trend. If you are looking at the market using a top down perspective, however, then the market strength is reversed and anything beneath the 1x1 angle is then considered a weak position.

Finally, Gann angles can also prove useful when it comes to determining key changes to the tops and bottoms of a given trend. This can be used as an indicator that change in a particular direction is imminent once the market reaches a point where time and price are moving apace with one another. This indicator is likely to be visible on the longer charts starting at the weekly range because it is common for daily charts to have a steady stream of bottoms and tops which can make them hard to reliably analyze in the long-term. The greater the angles of the cluster are, the more likely it is that their results will come to pass.

Double tops: The double top pattern is very easy to identify thanks to it pair of mountainous peaks that take up much of the timeframe. While the shape of the mountain can vary slightly the points of both peaks with remain virtually identical. When one peak is formed on a chart, it doesn't mean much, but when two peaks are formed on a chart, it means that investors have been selling a particular underlying asset, but it cannot be sold for a higher price than what is indicated on the chart. When you see two peaks, it means that people are likely going to stop buying the underlying asset in question.

As such, if you find yourself looking at this type of chart you will want to find an entry point that is just below the peaks as this is likely where the price will end up sooner than later. This chart pattern is typically quite destructive as it will cause many investors to change up their strategy in the short-term.

Double bottoms: Like the double tops, the double bottoms can be quite disruptive to the market as a whole. Unlike the double tops, it tends to cause most investors to take a long-term approach. The peaks will form in much the same way, but they will be situated at the lower part of the chart rather than near the top. While the first bottom can indicate to an investor that an uptrend might occur, the second bottom provides enough insight that a rise in price is very likely.

When a savvy investor sees this type of chart activity, he or she will likely position their investment at a price that is around the neckline of the peak. In addition to the two bottoms, the neckline is also an important aspect of this chart pattern because it is able to indicate to an investor that the price has not trended past that point for some time. For this reason, keeping the price around the neckline is a good idea, at least until a greater upward trend becomes apparent.

Ascending triangle: This pattern typically forms during an upward trend and indicates that the current pattern is going to continue. It is a bullish pattern that says greater growth and volume are on the way. It can also be formed during a reversal, signaling the end to a downward trend.

Descending triangle: This is similar to the ascending triangle but is bearish rather than bullish. It indicates that the current downward trend is likely to continue. It can occasionally be seen during a reversal but is much more likely to be a continuation.

Bullish triangle: This is a symmetrical triangle pattern that can be easily determined by a pair of trendlines that converge at a point. The lower trendline tracks support while the upper tracks resistance. Once the price breaks through the upper line then you know that a breakout has occurred that will rapidly pick up both steam and volume.

Rounded bottom: This pattern tracks a prolonged drop in price that will eventually rebound back to the point where it started. After the rebound occurs a reversal and breakout is likely to occur though it is best avoided as the new trend is likely not going to be strong enough to suit your day trading purposes.

Flag continuation: This pattern forms a rectangle with the support and resistance lines remaining parallel to one another. The slope of the parallel is likely to move counter to the original price movement. The point where the price breaks through can signal a strong indicator to buy or sell based on the direction of the breakout.

Bearish triangle: This triangular pattern is easy to identify because the support and resistance lines converge in a downward slope. The breakout point is always going to be on the support side and indicates a strong downward trend is forming that is likely to pick up volume significantly as it goes along.

Falling pennant: This pattern looks a lot like a triangle pattern except it doesn't quite come to a point. The trendlines will connect several peaks and valleys and once the breakout occurs it is likely that the price will move sharply in the direction of the breakout.

Chapter 6:

Money Management Tips

While choosing the right strategies, stocks and indicators is important, money management is also a crucial factor when it comes to successfully investing in the stock market in the long-term. Despite your most judicious efforts, if you aren't careful you can find yourself blowing through your initial trading capital without having anything substantial to show for it. Luckily, there are plenty of things you can do to ensure that your money ends up as safe as possible regardless of the type of trading you prefer.

Never allow your losses to multiply: When you are a new trader, it can be extremely easy to find yourself emotionally invested in the stocks you choose which is why you are going to need to learn to separate your expectations about a specific trade from the reality of what takes place once your money is committed in a specific way. To successfully ensure that you don't lose more than the bare minimum on a given trade it is important that you cut it lose the second it stops generating a profit as opposed to hanging on to it in hopes that it turns around and rebounds in the correct direction.

This means that one of the first things that you are going to need learn is that having a single failed trade is in no way a reflection on your skill as a trader, rather, it is simply a part of the trading process as natural as any other. Sticking with a losing trade is practically never going to be the best way to get that trade to turn around, and even if it does the odds are good that there will still be better ways that you could have put that money to use over the same period of time. This is why you are never going to want to double down on a losing trade in hopes of improving the odds of a potential loss. Adding to a losing position is similar to trying to dig yourself out of a hole, it is impossible, plain and simple.

Don't trade just to trade: When you are first getting used to trading on a regular basis, it can be easy to feel as though if you aren't trading then you are missing out, regardless of the quality of trades presented to you in the moment. The key takeaway here, is that quality is going to win out over quantity every single time. Making changes to your holdings or making trades just to trade is only going to decrease your profit margins, at best, or teach you bad habits, at worst. This can occur if this haphazard strategy pays off for you early on, causing you to double down on it moving forward and costing you far more in the long run than you can ever hope to gain from the practice in the first place.

Instead, it is always going to be a better choice to leave things as they are and wait for something truly worthwhile to come along before you go ahead and make your move. While there are some strategies that rely on a constant stream of trades, even those that are all chosen with care. Extra trades mean additional opportunities for loss, plain and simple, and poorly researched trades mean the potential for extra loss on top of that as well. With these types of odds, it is easy to see why this type of trading can be detrimental to your success in both the short and the long-term.

Choosing the right trades: Successful traders are always going to take a measured approach to the market, no matter what. To ensure that you always start out in the right way you are going to want to ensure that you choose the types of underlying assets that naturally align with your trading temperament, as well as your long-term goals.

Additionally, you are going to want to take all of the external knowledge you have on the topic into account when it comes to choosing a specific segment of the market to focus on. As an example, if you were previously in the medical field then stocks based on pharmaceutical companies might be a good choice. Regardless, it is important to always take the following three main aspects of every trade into account before you make any decisions.

First and foremost, it is important to choose a timeframe that you are comfortable with as going with a specific timeframe just because you believe it will be more profitable is a poor choice in the long run. Making this mistake can easily lead you to trading in scenarios where you are at less than your best because you are nervous, or simply impatient for something to happen.

If you are still trying to improve your overall trade percentage, you will likely want to stick to the 5-minute charts until you can be truly comfortable dealing with the potential for risk that holding stocks overnight can cause. You will also need to consider if you prefer micromanaging trades all day every day or prefer doing all of your research over the weekend to pursue weekly trades come Monday morning. Micromanaging trades leads to short-term gains while weekly trades produce long-term gains.

If you are up in the air as to which trading methodology is for you, it is important to focus on the things that work best for you as opposed to bouncing around to every single thing discussed in the book without taking the time to determine if they are actually working for you or not. It is important to keep in mind that every trader is going to have bad days, not matter how successful they are and switching your methodology constantly will only make it more difficult for you to determine where exactly you went wrong.

Much like methodologies, it is important to find a few trading instruments that work for you and focus on making the most of them. This is preferable to using a little bit of everything as you will be able to more closely tailor what you use to match your trading style. The best way to determine what is going to be useful to your style is by focusing on instruments that match the timeframes you frequent most often.

Keeping everything in mind at once can be difficult, but if you never put what you learn into practice then all of your hard work will never amount to anything in the first place. What's worse, you will never see much of a profit either. Once you get a handle on things you will then want to start keeping track of trades, from start to finish, so that you will always be on top of things in case they go south, and you find yourself having to jump ship to avoid losing all of your profits. It is important to remember that a small loss in the moment is always preferable to a big loss in the future.

Learning the most intricate parts of the markets you favor isn't something that can be taught, it can only be learned with practice. What's more, sometimes mood is going to skew unexpectedly and through everything out the window for a time. Ultimately it all comes down to Warren Buffet's number one rule, "the only hard and fast rule is to never lose money." Stick to this rule and you can never go wrong.

Portfolio Theory

Modern portfolio theory state that there is a specific way that risk-adverse investor can arrange their portfolios in such a way that they can maximize their expected returns based on the current state of the market and their desire for a specific level of risk. This theory posits that it is possible to construct what is known as an efficient frontier which is a tool which is used to posit the best possible return that can be expected from a given portfolio based on the amount of risk you are comfortable with. This theory was created by a man named Harry Markowitz and first published in the Journal of Finance in 1952.

One of the most important parts of this theory is that the returns that a particular investment sees, as well as its individual characteristics are best viewed, not in a vacuum, but in a way that takes into account all the various types issues that could affect the risk and return of the investment in question. It further stipulates that an investor can create a portfolio that is comprised of multiple assets that will, in turn, minimize risk or maximize profit as needed. This determination is based on statistical measures including correlation, variance and assumes that your return is less important than the ways in which the investment behaves when compared to the entire portfolio.

Rate of return expected: Modern portfolio theory assumes that every investor is naturally risk adverse to the point that they will only take on new risk if they are expecting greater return in the long run. As such, the return expected can then be found based on the weighted sum of the individual returns of various types of assets that would ideally be in the portfolio in question. For example, if a portfolio contains four different assets that are all equally weighted with returns of 4 percent, 6 percent, 10 percent and 14 percent then the expected return would work out to be:

(4x25)+(6x25)+(10x25)+(14x25) which equals 850 or 8.5 percent

Efficient frontier: The risk of the portfolio is then complicated by the variance of each asset along with any relevant correlations related to the specific assets in question. In order to calculate the risk of a four-asset portfolio correctly you would then need to take into account the level of variance along with the correlation values of each.

This is where the efficient frontier comes into play as every possible combination of assets can be plotted onto a graph that includes the risk on the x axis and the anticipated return on the y axis. This plot will then serve to reveal the most desirable outcomes when it comes to portfolio allocation. As an example, Portfolio A has an expected return set at 8.5 percent with a standard deviation of 8 percent while Portfolio B has the same expected return but a standard deviation of 9.5 percent.

As such, the first portfolio can be said to be more efficient for your needs while also sticking to a lower level of risk overall. This means that if you were to map out these investments you would want the result to map to a hyperbola that slopes upward. If it doesn't then you can safely assume it is time you reevaluated some of your investment decisions.

Kelly Criterion

Another popular money management method is known as the Kelly Criterion method. It was developed by an engineer named John Kelly while he was working for Bell Laboratory in an effort to decrease the amount of static that was heard on long distance telephone calls. However, it gained lasting fame when the investing community learned of it a realized it is also an efficient way of maximizing long-term investment holdings.

There are two main components to this system, the first is known as win probability which is the likelihood that a given trade is going to return a positive return in either the short or the long-term. Additionally, you will need to pay attention to the win/loss ration which can be found by simply taking the total number of positive trade amounts and then dividing them by the number of negative trade amounts in play over the same period of time. With these two numbers in hand, you simply plug them into this equation:

Kelly percent = W-[(1-W)/R]

In this instance, W equals the winning probability and the R equals with result of the win loss ratio. The result is the Kelly Percentage.

Using the Kelly percentage: To take advantage of this system, you will want to start by accessing your last 30 or 40 trades. You will then want to start by taking the number of successful trades that you have made by the total number of all the trades that you made. Ideally you want a number that is as close to 1 as possible. Any number over .5 is considered acceptable. This number is the W in the above equation.

From there you will just need to determine your win/loss ratio which can be found by simply taking the average gain from a specific number of trades and then dividing that by the average number of losses you saw within those same trades. Assuming your gains exceeded your losses, you will then end up with a result that is greater than 1. This will be the R in the Kelly equation. With this number in hand you will then be able to easily determine the Kelly Percentage of your profits.

Taking advantage of the results: The results from your personalized equation will ideally result in a number that is less than 1 which represent the total size of the positions that you will want to take on a regular basis in order to see a profit. As an example, if the Kelly percentage you came up with is .05 then you will want to take a 5 percent position on any of the equities in your portfolio. Essentially what this system does is let you know how much you need to diversify.

The system is not without a need for common sense, however, as regardless of what it says it is never a good idea to commit more than 25 percent of your available investment capital into a single equity. This amount is a greater risk than most investors can justify making.

This is purely a mathematical system that works based on potential growth for a set period of time. You can graph your own Kelly percentage using any equity chart graphing software. All results assume that you can keep up your current level of success indefinitely which should be reasonable assuming you stick to your personalized trading plan. This is not to say that the results will be 100 percent accurate, however, as no money management system is perfect, and the limitations of the system come into play when it still relies on you to pick trades that have a reasonable chance at success and also always trade in a reasonable manner.

Conclusion

Thank you for making it through to the end of Analysis Trading: All You Need to Know to Be Successful, let's hope it was informative and able to provide you with all of the tools you need to achieve your trading goals, whatever it is that they may be. Just because you've finished this book doesn't mean there is nothing left to learn on the topic, however, expanding your horizons is the only way to find the mastery, and the profits, that you seek.

Trading based on technical and fundamental analysis is one of the most complex, and potentially rewarding, types of trading a person can do. As such, it is only natural that at this point your head is spinning with all of the different potential options you can use to take your trading game to the next level regardless of the type of assets you favor. Nevertheless, it is important to start slow, and to ensure that you take your time to find the options that really work for you before you get carried away with more complicated options.

It can be easy to try and adopt too many new strategies at once, only to find that you have a hard time pinpointing the reasons that things didn't go according to plan when the worst happens. Take detailed notes and don't be afraid to take your time and try things as needed, using a new strategy in the wrong scenario just to try it out won't help anyone. Trying to fit a square peg into a round hole has never worked and trading is no exception. Remember, the process is a marathon, not a sprint, which means that slow and steady is always going to win the race in the end.

Finally, if you found this book useful in any way, a review on Amazon is always appreciated!

Description

When it comes to investing successfully, the person who comes out ahead isn't the person with the most money, or the most luck, it is the person who has all the answers to the questions the market asks each and every day. The answers to questions regarding trend, volume, volatility and more are all available, as long as you know the right questions to ask. If you are in a questioning mood, then Analysis Trading: All You Need to Know to Be Successful is the book you have been waiting for.

When it comes to ensuring that your successful trade percentage only increases as time goes on, you may find it useful to analyze the fundamentals of a company along with its technical aspects in order to determine if an investment is worthwhile. This is where technical and fundamental analysis come into play as fundamental analysis works to determine the underlying value of a given security through a focus on the things that affect a company's future prospects as well as its day to day business while technical analysis studies past market trends with the goal of accurately predicting those that are likely to occur again in the future.

Inside you will learn the secrets of using both successfully to maximize your potential profits, regardless of your chosen investment strategy. So, what are you waiting for, get ready to maximize your successful trade percentage and buy this book today!

Inside you will find

- Everything you ever wanted to know about the basics of fundamental and technical analysis, two great tastes that taste great together.
- Useful indicators for a wide variety of positive and negative trends.
- Candles for every occasion
- Money management tips

www.ingramcontent.com/pod-product-compliance
Lightning Source LLC
Chambersburg PA
CBHW070208230526
45471CB00002B/870